DESIGNER
SCRAPBOOKS
WITH *Dena*

DESIGNER SCRAPBOOKS

WITH *Dena*

Scrapbooking Style for
Pages, Parties & More

STERLING PUBLISHING CO., INC. NEW YORK
A STERLING/CHAPELLE BOOK

Chapelle, Ltd.
P.O. Box 9252, Ogden, UT 84409
(801) 621-2777 • (801) 621-2788 Fax
e-mail: chapelle@chapelleltd.com
Web site: www.chapelleltd.com

Editor: *Jennifer Gibbs*
Book Design: *Rose Sheifer*
Photography: *Ryne Hazen, Zak Williams*
Copy Editor: *Marilyn Goff*
Production Assistant: *Heidi Van Winkle*
Production Designer: *Ryan Christensen*

Library of Congress Cataloging-in-Publication Data

Fishbein, Dena.
Designer scrapbooks with Dena / [Dena Fishbein].
    p. cm.
"A Sterling/Chapelle Book."
Includes index.
ISBN 1-4027-2381-4
1. Photograph albums. 2. Photographs--Conservation and
restoration. 3. Scrapbooks. I. Title.

TR465.F57 2006
745.593--dc22

                                         2005024731

10 9 8 7 6 5 4 3 2 1
Published by Sterling Publishing Co., Inc.
387 Park Avenue South, New York, NY 10016
©2006 by Dena Fishbein
Distributed in Canada by Sterling Publishing
c/o Canadian Manda Group, 165 Dufferin Street
Toronto, Ontario, Canada M6K 3H6
Distributed in the United Kingdom by GMC Distribution Services,
Castle Place, 166 High Street, Lewes, East Sussex,
England BN7 1XU
Distributed in Australia by Capricorn Link (Australia) Pty. Ltd.
P.O. Box 704, Windsor, NSW 2756, Australia
Printed and Bound in China
All Rights Reserved

Sterling ISBN-13: 978-1-4027-2381-0
        ISBN-10: 1-4027-2381-4

For information about custom editions, special sales, premium
and corporate purchases, please contact Sterling Special Sales
Department at 800-805-5489 or specialsales@sterlingpub.com.

Contents

Introduction

I'm going to tell you a little secret. I wasn't always a scrapbooker. Though I've been an artist for over twenty years and have designed everything from greeting cards to bedding, I didn't fully understand what a pure pleasure scrapbooking is until recently. Sure, I had dabbled a little, making a page here or there. But I wasn't hooked until I finished my first major scrapbook project—a theme album—and found that I couldn't wait to get started on another. And another. And—you get the point. I'd start one project and ideas for more would rush into my head. It was like learning a new language; suddenly, I dreamed in paper.

Everything about the art of scrapbooking is enjoyable. The techniques and materials are unbelievably versatile. Not only can you use those treasured vintage buttons and bits of broken jewelry, you get to work with luscious papers and ingenious tools. And while scrapbooking is a delightful way to express your creativity, it's also a chance to refresh your spirit by thinking about the people and events you value. When you make a page, you remember every detail of a photograph and the story that surrounds it. When you make a card or a gift, you put something of yourself into it. Each detail of scrapbooking takes thought, and all those thoughts connect you more closely to the people you care about.

This book is the result of my newfound obsession. Since I design for a living, I couldn't help but develop an extensive line of scrapbook materials in the colors and patterns I love, so that I could make the projects as I saw them in my mind. From retro geometrics to vintage florals and everything in between, I aimed for the playfully chic look that makes me feel good. As I went along, the line grew to include coordinated and transparent papers, border design sheets, mini album kits, alphabets, sentiments—you name it. Colorbök partnered with my company to manufacture the line and sent me sample versions right away so I could use them for the projects featured here.

Marriage is a door which looks out upon a beautiful view. As that door is opened and the horizon unfolds before you, know that nothing is sweeter than the warmth of one hand within another.

—McCarty

It was a pure pleasure to create the scrapbook pages, albums, greeting cards, party decor, gifts, and other projects in this book. I am happy to share them and my newfound love for the amazing and versatile art of scrapbooking.

How I Got Started

People often ask how I became a designer, and I've often said I fell into it completely by accident. As a kid I loved making things like cardboard villages and stuffed animals from my own patterns, but when I went to UCLA, I didn't think of a career in designing decorative objects. Instead, I studied Landscape Architecture and Industrial Design.

After graduation, I decided to take a year off and moved to New York City with Danny, the love of my life, husband, and best friend. Thumbing through the Classifieds one day, I came across an ad for a textile designer and decided to apply. In college, I'd done numerous mechanical drawings of things like close-ups of eye-droppers and the inner workings of machines. It was all straight lines and rulers, nothing at all like the playful intuitive drawings that would become my specialty. I needed some supplies, so I went into the art store and said, "What do I use?" It was pathetic.

On the clerk's recommendation, I bought some gouache and a teeny tiny brush. Over the weekend, I painted a number of designs on squares of watercolor paper. On Monday morning, I tucked the drawings between the pages of a note-book and marched myself down to the agency that had placed the ad. Not only was this my first experience with an agency, it was my first job interview, ever. I was terrified. I walked around the block four times before I got up the nerve to go in. The waiting room was packed with designers looking intensely professional holding their big black portfolios—and there I was with my little notebook.

When my name was called, I stepped into an office to meet with a young woman. She looked at my little drawings, said she liked what she saw, and suggested I do more using fall colors. I rushed home and painted more designs in aqua, tangerine, and brown. She sold one to a European fabric manufacturer for maybe two hundred dollars. I was ecstatic.

While this was the very beginning of my design career, I didn't really know how committed I was until I had another interview, this time with a textile firm. Now I

had a big black portfolio like everyone else, and though I was nervous, it didn't take me four times around the block to go in. The person behind the desk, however, was more than intimidating—she was abrupt to the point of rudeness. She glanced at my drawings, said, "That's not the kind of thing we do here," and walked out of her office. No good-bye, no "Thanks for coming in." She simply left me standing there like a goofball.

And that's when I had my epiphany. I could wilt. I could quit. I could feel bad about my work. But I didn't. Instead, I simply thought, "I can do this." Despite that woman's attitude, I liked the design business and thought I could be successful in it whether or not people like her agreed.

So although it's true that my career began by chance, that's not the entire story. The whole story is that when an opportunity presented itself, I chose to work hard, take risks, overcome my fears, and persist in the face of obstacles (even prune-faced ones). Serendipity followed by a strong work ethic creates luck. It's this belief that has led me to the rewarding life of sharing my designs for a living—a life I wouldn't trade for the world.

Dena Designs, Inc.

During that first year in New York, I had the good luck to have my designs featured on the covers of two high-exposure catalogs. Afterward, manufacturers started calling my agent and I made the switch from selling work piece by piece to doing licensing agreements. I got a licensing agent, started Dena Designs, and eventually returned to California.

Keeping the company small was a deliberate choice. Over the years, Danny and I were blessed with three children and I didn't want work to prevent me from being there for them. I gained a lot of experience working with different types of companies doing many different projects during those years, and I loved working from home—still do. My studio is where the kids come in to do their homework and catch up after school, where we do projects together, and even where we eat occasionally. (You can read more about my studio in the book *Where Women Create.*)

As the kids grew, so did the company. In recent years, Dena Designs has gone from being a two-person business to an operation with several employees. In some ways, this move has been liberating for the artist in me. After all, I used to have to handle the contracts, lawyers, negotiations, and everything else in addition to creating my designs. Now I can focus on my strengths. Yet it's challenging, too. Being responsible for employees puts added pressure on the work I do and decisions I make. It matters to me that Dena Designs is a good place for them to work. I'm also committed to ensuring that our customers continue to receive the same level of attention from me that they always have and that nothing leaves the studio until I've approved it personally.

From an artistic standpoint, being able to focus almost exclusively on the creative side of the business means I create at a much faster pace. Luckily, this means that instead of running out of ideas, I have more and more. Maybe this is because I don't have the luxury to wait for inspiration. When it's time to work, I just go into the studio and start sketching. Sometimes I'll just jot down the name of a mood or of colors. Then I jump into working on my final design. After all, why wait? There are so many designs, so many great projects, just waiting to be discovered.

Art and Life

It's funny. Though I'd never painted a thing until I saw that ad in the paper, painting is now an integral part of my life. Whether I'm in the grocery store or at the beach, I'm always looking around and thinking about what colors and patterns go well together, and how to bring that into my work. My first question to Danny in a restaurant isn't "What are you getting?" It's "What would you change about this decor?"

I love working with colors; discovering new combinations is a lot of fun. I've always been drawn to the edge of what's popular, aiming to combine colors people like but in ways they might not have considered. It's a lot like finding new ways to use your materials, as you'll see with many of the projects in this book. I suspect that everyone has the ability to develop a unique style; it's a matter of taking the time to develop it by taking chances and trusting yourself.

Technique

As I've said, when I started my design career, I had no clue how to paint. I just got some supplies and figured it out as I went along. Over the years, I've learned from other artists. For instance, I no longer paint huge backgrounds with the same teeny brush I use for details. On the other hand, I've given myself permission to figure out my own approach, which includes inking details with the drafting pen I used in my mechanical drawing days. And though other textile designers often switch from acrylics to oils, to colored pencils, to computers, it's always been gouache for me.

There was a time when I considered learning how to draw like other textile designers. I almost signed up for a class, but Danny pointed out that people were responding to the unusual, naïve look of my approach. I'm glad I took his advice. Because I didn't bind myself to the same rules other designers were following, my style was my own. And I liked that it seemed loose and hand-painted rather than perfect. To me, there's a warmth and an energy to the look.

When it comes to doing scrapbooking, the same philosophy I hold for drawing prevails. It's good to be open to other people's ideas, but the best way to learn is to pick materials you want to spend time with and get to work. You make mistakes, change your mind, and stumble onto brilliant answers to questions you didn't even know you had. It's a process, and with every new project, your skills grow. In my opinion, it's not a bad thing if your projects look handcrafted rather than professional. After all, it's your unique way of putting things together that makes them more personal—and more valuable.

To create each scrapbook project in this book, I began by selecting a focal point (such as a photograph) and choosing a color palette to set the mood. Then I developed the layout and built the project. As I created dozens of scrapbook pages, my imagination reached for even more ways to use these great materials. Ideas for gifts, accessories, and storage solutions filled my head; and soon I wanted to create whole experiences that had the same rich, lovingly made feel of a scrapbook page. This led to the concept of the parties you'll see here. To me, designing a party is like designing a page; you select a focal point or theme and build out from there, coordinating things like invitations, favors, and decor.

The result of this undertaking is more than one hundred projects. My deepest hope is that they'll inspire you to try new scrapbooking challenges, whether this means trying new materials and layouts or inventing your own "off-the-page" ways to create special memories with your scrapbooking skills.

Dena

Treat people as if they were what they ought to be and you help them to become what they are capable of being.

Goethe

Dana

We loved

with a

love that

was more

than love.

Edgar Allan Poe

Happiness is being with you
—Unknown

La Mode®

diva

Let us celebrate the occasion with wine and sweet words.
— Plautus

Our Wedd

I love you

Happy Birthday

Though we travel the world over to find the beautiful, we must carry it with us or we find it not.
—Ralph Waldo Emerson

hope

tender moments

sister

We loved with a love
that was more than love.
Edgar Allan Poe

Scrapbook Pages

There's no right or wrong way to build a scrapbook page—what pleases you is what is most important. I like to develop pages that I think work well when put together in an album. Sometimes this means repeating elements such as a certain type of embellishment, color scheme, or layout to provide continuity from page to page. Other times it means alternating standard with interactive pages, or pastels with brights.

La Mode

memories

gentle

gentle words

Party Time Present

In this layout, a present of pretty, festive paper hides a surprise. When you lift the box to see a special photo and sentiments, it's almost like getting a gift.

See project instructions on page 136.

Harry

Grandma Terry's birthday yielded lots of fun photos, including this one of Lisa holding Uncle Andy's beloved Jack Russell terrier in a full nelson.

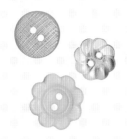

Together

To create a look that balances Danny's masculinity with baby Rachel's femininity, I relied on graphical stripes and polka dots in colors ranging from delicate pastels to strong black. The pocket tag holds a message to Rachel from Danny.

Amazing Girl

The graphical layout of this page allows you to have the best of both worlds: a rich layering of delicate elements and the quiet drama of a photograph in its own space. Gentle pastels complement the baby's coloring without pulling attention away from where it belongs—on the amazing girl herself.

Me and My Mom

Sometimes the simplest designs have the most impact. By keeping the stronger color at the borders, this layout draws the eye to the photo, which is particularly special to me because a family friend, photographer David Gahr, took it.

Sweet Girl

I was taken by surprise at how sentimental I felt creating this mixed media collage page. Though my oldest daughter is a teenager now, there's a corner of my heart where she'll always be nine months old.

Grandma Sophie

Every family has at least one magnificent cook, and Grandma Sophie was ours. One of my paper collections includes blank recipe cards like those you see here with a hand-lettered recipe for Grandma's Mandel Brote Cookies.

Family

The classic look of a black-and-white portrait is enhanced by the simplicity of this color scheme. Visual interest is created while keeping the focus on the photo with two shades of blue paper, a covered mat for texture, and a hint of pink with a die-cut border.

Loving You

My youngest, Lisa, and our dog Buddy. I love that they're both smiling. To me, the ribbon woven through hole-punched "frame" adds a touch that is sweet without being saccharin—like the two characters in the photo.

Loving You

childhood
is the most
beautiful
of all life's
seasons.

Rachel posing for Darla
in the front garden.

happiness

Happiness

When a patchwork of patterns is made from colors that blend together well, it offsets a black-and-white image beautifully. Create balance on the page while drawing the eye to the photo, with the thoughtful placement of vibrant color such as the pink floral paper at the edges of this layout.

Best Friends

It's crucial to celebrate sisterhood's closest moments. A paper flower, woven sentiment labels, and a double mat gives this page a rich texture while the colors and patterns say "All Girl."

Make a Wish

Multiple photos can gesture toward the story that surrounds them. I'll never forget this day.
The kids had Danny and me striking silly poses while playing photo shoot in a Washington park.
Later, we drove through an animal preserve where a buffalo stuck its enormous head in our car.
We all ended up laughing a lot on that vacation.

Memories

Kids love interactive elements in scrapbooks (and so do I). In this design, the pink flap of the purse goes up and the blue body of the purse flips down to provide extra space for photos.

Girlfriends

Rachel (on the right) plays dress-up with friends Lizzy and Abby. Page accents such as the ribbon laced on the left border repeat colors in the photo, and the background paper reinforces the dress-up theme, bringing a sense of unity to the layout.

Purse Dog

Our little dog Ruby is already adorable, so I wanted a design that would be cute but not too cute. I think the brown of the purse, striped background, and metal belt buckle balances the sweetness of pink ribbon accents, velvet bow, and Ruby's little face. The purse itself is a pocket for additional photos, journal pages, and other doggy memorabilia.

Forever

At first, I intended to simply embellish a mat and frame this photo of Danny and me, but I like how it looked as a scrapbook page. Repeated elements such as shell buttons and crimped paper keep the page from becoming too busy.

Getting Married

Including some pages without photos in your scrapbook can make it more interesting. Tuck treasured items such as wedding invitations into an embellished pocket.

Two Ladies

Two photographs, one page. In this layout, each photo receives a place of honor when surrounded by a unique frame and sentiment. Repeated elements such as pink paper flowers and buttons maintain a sense of unity in the design.

Old and New

For a fresh approach to enhancing vintage photos, choose contemporary elements that gesture toward rather than replicate a by-gone era. Here, pink pinstripes recall the fabric of a seersucker jacket the gentleman may have worn, while new ribbon trim frames the lady in the upper corner.

Our First Trip to Japan

To me, the vibrant colors and playful images on this page catch the energy of the adventures Danny and I had on a trip to Japan. Belt straps made from faux leather paper and a dangling tag create a multidimensional look. The suitcase flips up to reveal photos of our journey.

Celebrate the Moments

Catch the gentle side of masculinity with a strong graphic layout, simple aqua/black palette, and combination of understated stripes and dots. Here, my son David rescues a squirrel that fell from a tree.

Celebrate
the moments

David

rescues

a
baby squirrel

Albums and Mini Albums

Why limit your creativity to the pages inside a scrapbook when the cover begs for embellishment, too? Creative ways to announce an album's theme and delight the imagination range from simple touches to elaborate designs. Here are some of my personal favorites.

Purse Album #1

When designing a cover, consider how simply turning the album on its side opens up a number of possibilities. Here, an album becomes a purse when its spine becomes the top and a real purse handle is added.

See project instructions on pages 136–137

Adorable Baby

Frame a favorite photo with a striped mat, add borders, sentiment, and ribbon closure, and you can have a baby album with almost as much personality as the baby herself.

Purse Album #2

Another variation on the purse theme, this album mixes textures and patterns for a fresh, feminine look.

Our Wedding Day Guest Book

Whimsical wedding paper, sparkling rhinestones, and paper flowers create a guest book or wedding album that's sure to please in the years to come.

Our Paris Album

One of my favorite places to travel to is Paris. The history, the romance— the shopping. I love it so much that I created an album just for photos of this special place. To make your own travel album, cut a suitcase from scrapbook paper and a handle from vinyl, and add whatever tags and letters you need.

Homemade Recipes Album

Holiday dinner menus, favorite desserts, Uncle Rob's Secret Barbecue Sauce. Keep all of them together beautifully in a specialty album.

Home Sweet Home Album Cover

You don't need a lot to create great album covers. Find one embellishment you love, add borders to the top and bottom edges, and you can have an album that's sweet, simple, and utterly delightful.

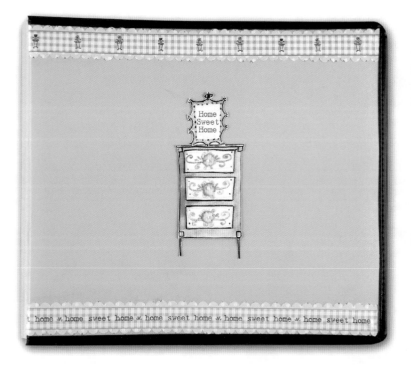

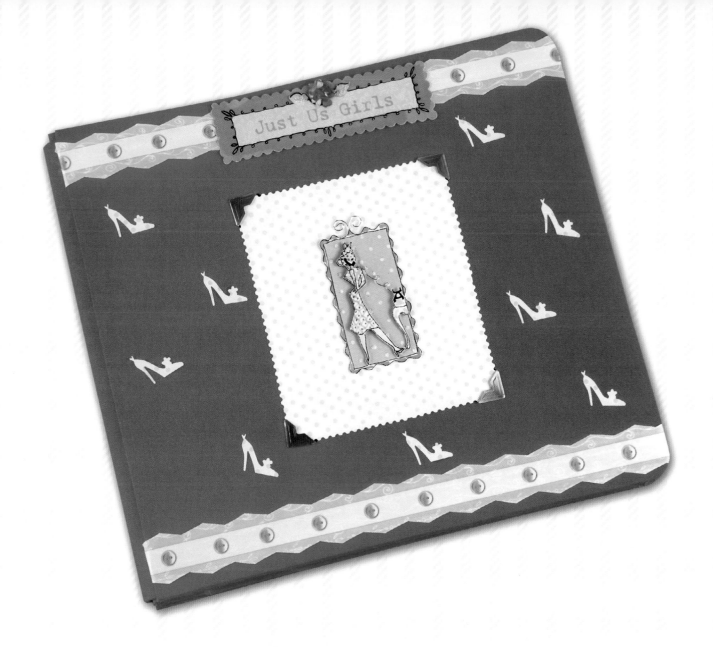

Just Us Girls

To me, hot pink is unapologetically feminine; so to decorate this album, I punched shoes from scrapbook paper, added a blue border, and set a hip little embellishment in the center. Voila! An album perfect for pages from an old diary, photos of girlfriends, and maybe even a high school love letter or two.

Holiday Album

The window of a die-cut album cover begs for a raised embellishment. Here, a strip of pink paper mounted down the center of green striped paper adds to the festive look.

Mini Albums

Need to make a great gift fast? Want a classy way to carry around favorite photos? Mini albums are the way to go. The smaller size means you can achieve beautiful effects in less time for an album that tucks easily into a purse or satchel. If you want to focus on creating rather than shopping, try a mini album kit that includes coordinating papers and embellishments, like the ones I used to create the designs you see here.

Happy

Flipping the pages of a mini album filled with moments to remember is a guaranteed pick-me-up for a busy day. Touches of lavender and aqua carry the design of the cover into the pages for a more unified feel.

Family

A mixture of stripes and florals create a look that's fresh yet traditional and will complement all sorts of photographs. A small collection of favorite family shots tucks easily into Grandma's suitcase or the duffle bag of a college-bound student.

Good Dog

Proud of your pet? Tame all those photos in a mini album that comes complete with cat and dog stickers.

New Baby

This mini album is sweet, playful, and oh-so-girlie. Fill with photos of your darling,
or give empty to a new mom or dad.

Sweet Dreams

Varied patterns make the simple blue-and-white palette as rich as it is sweet with a mini album for a baby boy. Experiment with layout to create a unique look when using a kit.

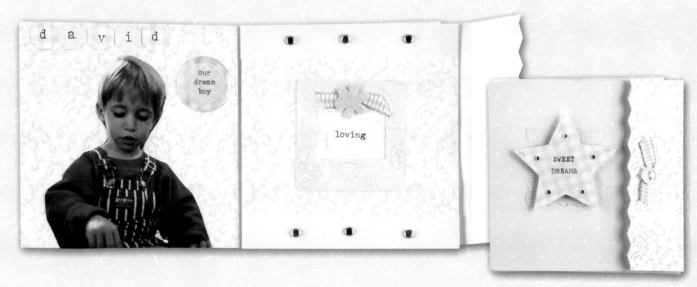

Happy Birthday

One of the things I love about a mini album is that it gives you a portable gallery for photos from a single event, such as a child's birthday party.

Retro Reindeer

Have hipsters on your Christmas list? Give them a gift that puts a spin on tradition. Here, red becomes pink and green becomes mint and aqua in a color scheme that looks perfect under a cool bottlebrush tree.

Picture Perfect Vacation

A mini album holds just the right number of photos to delight your friends with highlights of your vacation. Classic, sophisticated plaid always makes me think of log cabins and cool summer evenings in the woods.

My Friend

Pink and black always says chic to me—just right for a mini album that celebrates a special friendship.

Jolly

Fill this cheerful album with photos from all year 'round to give a faraway loved one a make believe visit during the holidays.

Wishing you a year
filled with love and joy.
Happy Birthday!

Birthday Wishes

We loved
with a
love that
was more
than love.

Greeting Cards

Tuck one under the bow of a present, set one on a breakfast plate, or slip one into the mail. A handmade greeting card is sure to win a smile, and when you see how easy these designs are to make, you'll want to give one to everyone you know.

Friendships

You're Invited

Cake Card

The secret to this simple birthday card design is to layer it like a cake with rich detail. It's a great opportunity to make use of those paper scraps and tiny embellishments you've been hanging onto.

See project instructions on pages 137–138.

Love Card

Pink and green is a color combination that brings the optimism of spring to any time of the year. This card was made with a Dena Designs kit that includes everything you need to create this look.

We loved

with a

love that

was more

than love.

Edgar Allan Poe

The Groom, The Bride Card

Images pop when you cut them out and "float" them over matching elements in a background, using foam dots and glitter accents.

Pocket Card

Repeated motifs bring together different elements of a card. Here, round holes punched along the pocket's borders echo the dots on the ribbon. When you open the card, the other side of the ribbon appears, adding to the overall effect.

Enjoy Card

You're only five minutes away from a great handmade card. A charming border punch and a ready-made embellished sentiment turn a piece of colored cardstock into a cheerful message to a friend.

It Takes a Long Time to Grow an Old Friend

Soft words carry a strong message when printed on vellum and offset by a gentle pastel background.
Here, a collage flower and pot add texture and richness.

It takes a long time to grow an old friend.

Birthday Wishes Card

A cheerful pink-and-green palette is enhanced by punch out borders, a single paper flower, and a die-cut cupcake to make this design appropriate for nearly everyone.

Wishing You a Year Full of Love Card

A border ribbon and a wallpaper-inspired pattern for the center square lend this design a vintage feel, while cut corners give the sentiment extra presence. A ready-made border in a playful design combines with the puppy to update the overall look, resulting in a cheerful blend of old and new.

Friendships Card

Dip into your button collection to add a unique element to your handmade cards. Here, a sparkly button set on a scrap of ribbon adds texture and showcases the sentiment below it.

Happy Birthday Card

The touch of plaid infuses this vintage-inspired design with contemporary flair in this Dena Designs card kit.

Everyday Card

Make someone's day with this cheerful understated design. I made this card from die-cut cardstock, but you can achieve this effect, using a square punch. Pick up the motif of the stamped shoe on the card with a stamped border on a ready-made envelope.

French Poodle Card

With four folds, this card can double as a mini album or just give you plenty of room for that nice long letter you've been meaning to write. The simplicity of the flirty puppy embellishment and stamped border means you'll have time to write that letter, too.

Calling Card

Stamps, tags, and little piece of ribbon make for simple but charming little cards you can hand to acquaintances or attach to gifts.

Glitter Dress Card

Enhance a simple image by floating it against a wash of color. To create this look, stamp a dress onto a small square of paper, drizzle glue along the edges, and dip them into glitter. Attach it to the card with a foam dot and stamp the top and bottom borders.

Cards and Envelopes

Lend an extra sense of occasion to any event by presenting friends with 5" x 5" cards nestled into lined envelopes. Use spray adhesive to attach two coordinating scrapbook papers and cut four rounded flaps. You can scallop the edge of the top flap and fold them closed around your card like the petals of a flower. Seal with a large sticker.

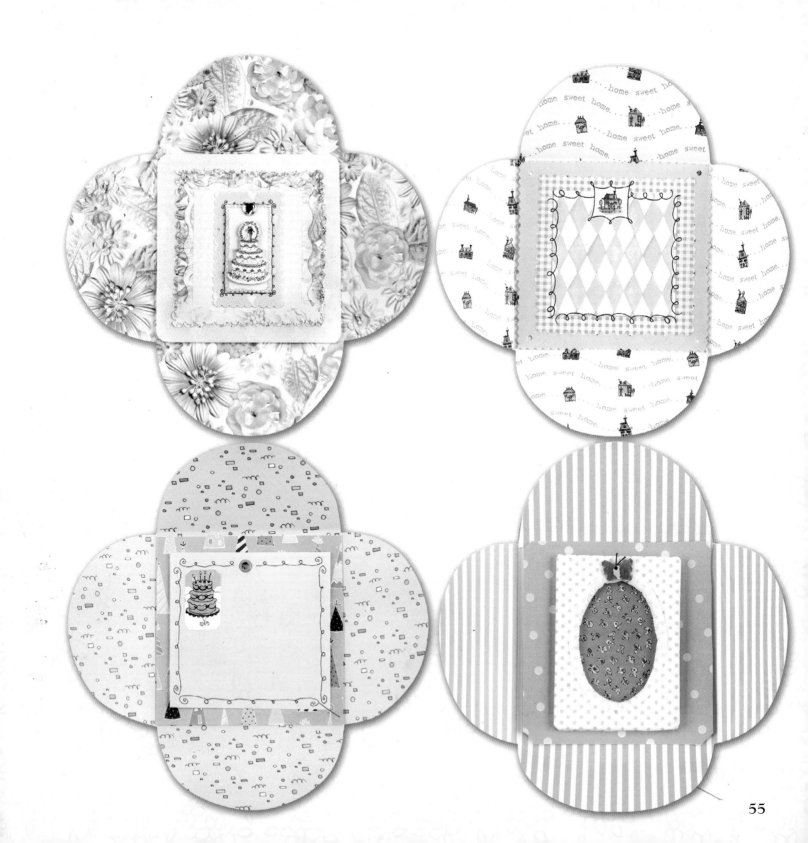

55

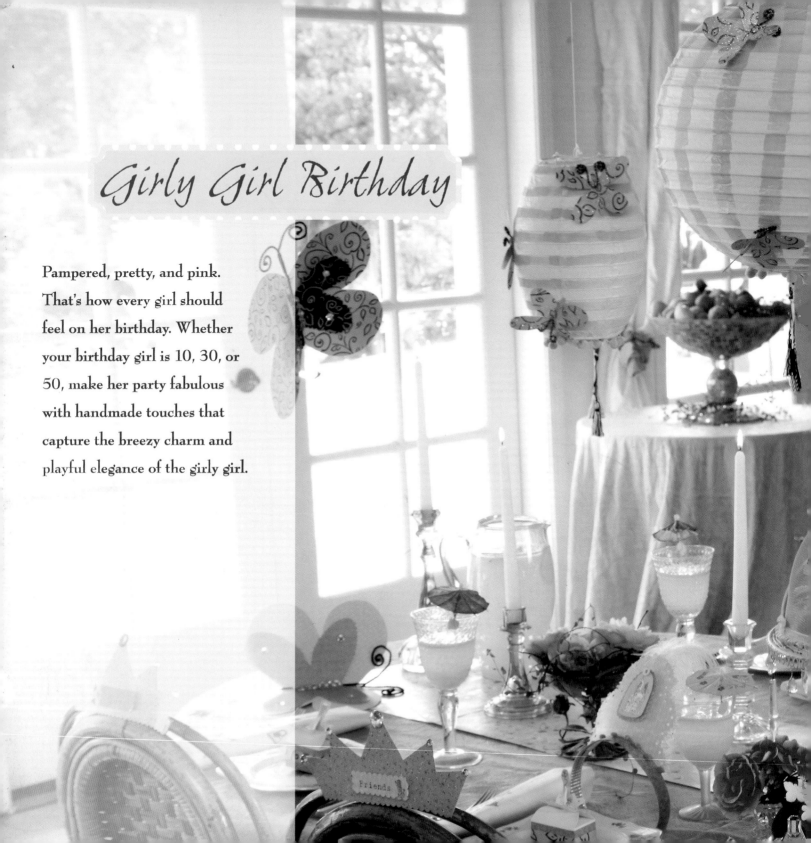

Girly Girl Birthday

Pampered, pretty, and pink.
That's how every girl should
feel on her birthday. Whether
your birthday girl is 10, 30, or
50, make her party fabulous
with handmade touches that
capture the breezy charm and
playful elegance of the girly girl.

Paper Purse Invitation

Your guest will smile when she opens a delightful invitation that looks like something Audrey Hepburn might have carried in *Funny Face*.

See project instructions on page 138.

Girly Girl Cupcake Toppers

Celebrate all things girly with easy-to-make cupcake toppers. To create, simply cut out fun images from scrapbook paper and mount them on extra long toothpicks with nontoxic glue. Add a pink pom-pom to each for an extra flourish.

Pom-pom Tiara

With a glamorous tiara on her head, how can your birthday princess think anything but gorgeous thoughts?

Sweet Boxes

Your guests will love party favor boxes into which you can tuck chocolates, earrings, or other treats.

Butterflies and Paper Lanterns

Hearts will lighten when your guests raise their eyes to see butterflies floating amidst inexpensive paper lanterns.

Valentine's Party

Infuse the depths of winter with the warmth and romance of a spectacular Valentine's Party. Whether you invite family, friends, or just that one sweetheart, these projects will help you make February 14th a day worth remembering.

Love Bar Party Favors

Your favorite chocolate bars become gorgeous favors guaranteed to suit all ages. Because this project takes little time, it's great for large or small parties.

See project instructions on page 139.

Valentine's Party Invitation

Charm your guest with an invitation that uses a heart shape in an unusual way. Here, a heart opens to reveal the party information. The business-envelope size also helps it stand out from all the other cards in the mailbox.

what: A Valentine's Party
when: February 14th 6:00pm
where: Rachel's house

R.S.V.P. Rachel

bring: supplies to make
Valentines

a Valentine dinner
will be served

Heart Petals

Scatter tiny paper hearts for a pretty, playful way to extend the party theme to every corner of the table.

Valentine Place Card

Hearts, flowers, and a touch of tulle make a lovely personal valentine and place card.

Glittery Hanging Hearts

Romance the air with beautiful glittery hearts. Layer one slightly smaller paper heart onto one cut from a coordinating paper. Scallop the edges, punch a hole in the center, and string from a ribbon or fishing line above your dining table.

Big Love
Cake Tower

Fill decorated round boxes with
cookies, candies, and petits fours; stack,
and top with a cupcake for a sumptuous
centerpiece. At dessert time, simply
scatter the boxes and lift the lids.

Bridal Shower

She's getting married. Now is
the time to begin the celebra-
tion of love, friendship, and the
future. Surround the bride with
lovingly made details she'll
cherish in her memories of this
special time in her life.

Bridal Shower Invitation

With a pastel umbrella and glittery details, what else could it be but a bridal shower invitation? Pink and seafoam green set a soft and romantic mood from the start.

Elegant Glass Plates

Set a beautiful table with plates made especially for the occasion. Simply sandwich photos, flowers, sentiments, or perhaps a poem between two glass plates. When the party is over, separate the plates, set aside the embellishments, and pop the plates in the dishwasher.

See project instructions on page 139.

Marriage is a door which
looks out upon a beautiful view.
As that door is opened and
the horizon unfolds before you,
know that nothing is sweeter
than the warmth of one
hand within another.

-McCarty

Embellished Soaps

Your guests will feel pretty as brides themselves
when they take home these charming favors.
Wrap sweet-smelling glycerin soaps in crimped
paper, overlay a decorative paper center, and
embellish with images cut from scrapbook paper
and a touch of glitter.

Wedding Dress
Centerpieces

Purchased papier-mâché dress forms let you focus
on the fun part of this project: creating the
dresses. Different papers and techniques make
each one unique. Attach a dowel to each form and
plant in a rich green bed of wheatgrass as shown
on page 70 for a gorgeous, unusual centerpiece.

Wedding Bells

Trim a gazebo with simple yet pretty paper bells
for a whimsically elegant shower *al fresco*.

Paper Placemats

Carry the fresh, festive look across the table with
placemats made from coordinating scrapbook
papers. Small but delightful touches such as paper
flowers and scalloped edges are easy to add.

Tasseled Fan

With the right paper, something as simple as a fan for each place setting can make an elegant statement.

Chair Embellishment

Decorating the chairs is a great way to pull together party decor—which is especially important to do when entertaining outdoors, where you don't have walls to help define the space. Spell the bride's name with letters on wedding dresses such as this one for an added personal touch.

Hello, Baby

Tender. Innocent. Delightful. A baby changes a new parent's world forever. Help your friend welcome the transformation into parenthood with a shower full of thoughtful touches that evoke the magic of all things baby.

Sweety Cups

Transform cold drink paper cups to match your unique decor with pretty handcrafted embellishments.

See project instructions on pages 139–140.

Baby Dear Invitation

The apron of this single-panel invitation lifts to reveal party information. Is the mom-to-be expecting a boy? Cut out overalls in blue or green with a flip-down bib.

A Baby Shower

For: Maisy Houston
when: Saturday June 8m
where: 4 Rose Lane
time: 11:30 A.M.
lunch will be served.

Thank-you Card

Give parents-to-be a pretty yet practical gift with a box of handmade cards for all those thank-yous they will have to write. This card features a tiny dress that hangs from miniature clothespins clipped to a real piece of string.

Baby Gift Box Tower

It's more than a centerpiece—it's a set of boxes you can fill with tiny gifts for Baby now, and Mom can fill with keepsakes later.

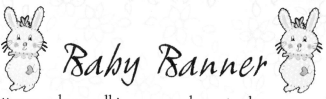

Baby Banner

Delightful pretty paper dresses all in a row can be as simple or as over-the-top as you like. If the baby's a boy, replace the dresses with paper overalls. Don't know yet? Alternate dresses and overalls or cut out onesies in yellow and green.

Baby Shower
Party Favor

Cover museum board cones with frilly paper,
add a ribbon, and fill with paper flowers.

Afternoon Spa

Soothing music, scented candles, and a room filled with luminous pastels turn a quiet afternoon at your home into an escape to a spa. Treat your friends to lunch served in decor that calms the spirit, pampers the body, and refreshes the soul.

Peaceful Blossom Centerpiece

Natural touches ground the spirit and delight the eye. Branches can bloom anytime of the year when you add scrapbook paper flowers in a delicate pink.

Recipe for Relaxation Envelope

To me, a room isn't really ready for a party until even the chairs are made part of the decor. This lovely chair embellishment is an envelope for cards on which you can print recipes for home-made facials, bath salts, and teas.

See project instructions on pages 140–141.

Recipe

Oat and brown sugar facial scrub

2 tbsp. ground oats
2 tsp. brown sugar
2 tbsp aloe vera,
1 tsp lemon juice
1 tsp fresh orange juice

Instructions:
Place rolled oats in a blender to grind the flakes
Into a fine powder

Mix the ingredients in a large bowl until the
consistency becomes a smooth paste. Massage
face gently

Soothing Soak Bath Salts

Pretty to look at and delightful to use, embellished bottles with scented bath salts let your friends bring the spa experience home. Salts can be purchased in bulk at many health food stores or made by combining sea salt, a few drops of lavender essential oil, and flecks of dried mint or orange peel.

A Touch of Decadence

It's been scientifically proven that pleasure is good for you—so encourage your guests to indulge in dessert with a gorgeous presentation. Add layers of scalloped and crimped borders to the edge of any cake plate, and embellish with bows. This display works equally well for serving sandwiches.

Spa Napkin Rings

Add an elegant spa touch to the table with napkin rings created to match your decor. To me, this color combination of pink, cream, and green are both soothing and refreshing at the same time.

Spa Afternoon Invitation

A flower blooms in the center of a serene background on this invitation to an afternoon of relaxing fun. The trim adds a playful note.

Aromatherapy Candleholders

Candles scented with essential oils of lavender, linden, and rose geranium are believed by some to calm the nervous system. Set in pretty candleholders like these, they're sure to create a soothing mood with their soft light and gentle colors.

Light as a Bubble Streamers

These streamers greet guests with colors and words that inspire a relaxed mood. To make, use a computer to print words such as "Relax" and "Enjoy," then glue to the center of circles cut from scrapbook paper. Glue the "bubbles" to a strip of ribbon and hang over the table with a long ribbon or fishing line.

Message Rocks

Something as simple as a stone can remind us to pause and appreciate the moment. Scattered across a table, stones bearing messages invite quiet contemplation.

tranquility

relax

soothing

bath

cleansing

serenity

spirit

relaxation

comfort

refresh

peace

calm

spa

Recipe Exchange Party

Grandma Sophie's recipe card box overflowed with instructions for creating mouth-watering treats. These days, it's easy to forget the loving care that goes into building a collection of treasured recipes. Why not make it easy for your friends to steal a couple of hours from their busy lives to share an evening of food, conversation, and favorite kitchen secrets? You'll feel nourished in more ways than one. If you'd like, you can even provide them with blank recipe cards to write on.

Recipe Exchange Invitation

The apron flips up to reveal party details. Request that guests bring a sample of their favorite finger food and the recipe for it written out. If you'd like, you can even provide them with a blank card to write on. When they R.S.V.P., be sure to ask what they intend to bring so you can include it on the Tasty Diner-style Menu.

Napkin Rings

Great party decor is in the details. These easy-to-make napkins rings with stylish retro tags add flair to your table.

See project instructions on page 141.

Tasty Diner-style Menu

Filled in with a list of the foods each guest will bring and set on the refreshment table, this menu acts both as a centerpiece and tasting guide.

Place Card Favors

Inexpensive mini frames from a craft store become charming one-of-a-kind gifts when you embellish them with scrapbook paper and hand-drawn borders. Attach a guest's name and a ribbon to use as place cards now; later, the guest can slip in a photo of the party.

Recipe Cards and Pencils

Scatter blank recipe cards on the table with pencils covered in coordinated paper so guests can copy recipes as they talk and eat. You can cut your own from cardstock or purchase ready-made. (The ones you see here are from one of my collections.)

Hanging Lanterns

Paper lanterns from an import store can be quickly converted to fit your theme. Simply replace the original paper with your own and hang above the table for a festive touch.

Cupcake Chair Embellishment

Remind your guests of the good things in life with fun and fanciful decor. Food-themed chair embellishments like these paper cupcakes fit the Recipe Exchange Party perfectly.

Chef's Hat

Your guests will want to get down to the serious business of having fun the moment you greet them wearing a paper chef's hat. Found easily at culinary stores, these hats can be embellished so quickly that you may want to make one for everyone.

Honey Pie Dessert Plate

Treats taste even better when served on a fancy plate. Here, a border of decorative papers has been embellished with rhinestones and cut-outs to give the table a little extra eye-candy.

Pinwheel Centerpiece

Too often, a party table is just a table. But plant giant pinwheels made from coordinated scrapbook papers in bowls of marbles, and your table will look great (no matter what containers your guests bring).

Doggie Party

If you're anything like me, your pet is part of the family—and if your family is anything like mine, they love to celebrate. When you want an excuse to turn an ordinary Saturday into a family event, why not throw a party in honor of one of your four-legged friends? You need just a few simple things, a little time, and a big sense of humor.

Dog Basket Centerpiece

This Scottie cutout turns any flat-sided container or basket into a whimsical focal point for the table. Fill the container with cookies for your two-legged guests.

See project instructions on pages 141–142.

Doggy Invitation

To convey the whimsical spirit of the Doggy Party, I chose papers in colors and patterns you don't usually see combined. The dog's red-and-white checkered jacket lifts to reveal information about the upcoming event.

Wrapped Dog Treats

Bring the party spirit to every detail—right down to the snacks you serve the dogs. Custom wrappers cut from scrapbook paper and sealed with nontoxic glue dress up the dogs' favorite treat.

Dog Banner

Nothing says "Party" to me like a decorative banner. Paper terriers spell out our special guest's name.

Playful Pennant

Easy-to-make paper flags strung across the room are another great way to fill the room with party cheer. Use alone or crisscross with the Dog Banner to add extra flair.

Party Hats

Have the camera ready when you set one of these toppers on the guest of honor's head. To make, simply cover a ready-made paper cone hat with Scottie paper and embellish with a bit of boa.

Bone Placemat

Cut dog-themed scrapbook paper into the shape of a bone to make placemats the perfect size for snack plates.

Doggy Bags

This doggy bag really is for the dog! Fill a plain paper lunch bag with dog biscuits or a new chew toy, fold closed, and embellish.

Gifts and Accessories

One of the things I love about scrapbooking is that the same techniques and materials you bring to your albums and pages can transform practically any-thing into a one-of-a-kind keepsake. Whether you want to embellish an object for a friend or your home, you hardly need to look further than your scrap-booking supplies.

Domed Photo Display

A clear glass bowl makes a unique setting for a photo in a project that's easier to make than it looks. For best results, select a bowl that has a flat rim and no printing or decoration on the bottom.

See project instructions on page 142.

Kitten Chocolate Bar

Create your own chocolate bar label to make a sweet gift even sweeter. Rubber stamps make this project quick and easy.

Christmas Stacked Boxes

Don't just give a gift—give an experience. Tiered round boxes covered with coordinated papers make a grand entrance or enticing display under a Christmas tree.

Napkin Rings

Dress up the table for any occasion with easy-to-make napkin rings. Tuck in a fresh flower or sprig of parsley or rosemary for added flair.

Maple Syrup Bottle

What tastes better than maple syrup? Maple syrup in an embellished bottle, of course. Add just a few simple touches and you have a hostess gift or wedding brunch item that's as sweet on the inside as it is on the outside.

Retro Oil and Vinegar Bottles

Customize store-bought bottles with images cut from scrapbook paper. Add sprigs of tarragon, rosemary, or other herbs and fill with oil and vinegar.

Gift Cans

Give inexpensive tins a designer touch with specialty papers. These make great hostess gifts when filled with candies or gourmet coffee.

Decorated Bottles

A shell, a paper cutout, a length of ribbon.
Small details adhered onto clear glass bottles
make a charming presentation for anything from
bubble bath to cocktail mixer.

Shell Jar

You can almost hear the ocean when you gaze at
delicate bone-white shells. With an inspirational
quote printed on vellum paper adhered to the
outside, this jar is ready to grace an office
desk or bathroom counter.

Though we travel the world over to find the beautiful we must carry it with us or we find it not.

Ralph Waldo Emerson

Custom CD Covers

Now that we can create our own song mixes to reflect every mood and occasion, it's time to make covers that match. Use the same techniques and materials you use for scrapbooking to make unique cover art for your special-occasion CDs.

Snow Globe Greetings

I used snow globes from a craft store that include a slot for photos to create these Christmas-themed stocking stuffers.

Tic-tac-toe Game

An old picture frame, transparent
cabochons, and coordinating scrapbook papers make a beautiful game
to set out on an occasional table.

Changing Table Jar

With a paper border around the top and delicate images glued to the sides, ordinary glass or acrylic jars become perfect for cotton balls, swabs, and other items that every baby's changing table needs.

Friendship Cloche

Readily available, glass cloches are ideal for containing and protecting small vignettes. To create this one, I cut a mat board base, covered it in moss, then added an enlarged clipart image, a branch from the garden, and details such as vintage flowers, a watch face, and a vellum sentiment.

Lampshade

A charming lamp base needs a shade to match. A little girl's lamp gets the perfect top when flat-bottomed pearls, paper flowers, and pretty scrapbook paper borders make a plain shade something special.

Charming Glass Vase

A decoupaged vase makes a bouquet to a friend that much more special. To use for fresh flowers, slip a smaller container for water into the embellished vase.

Daisy Photo Mat

Why send someone just a photo tucked into a card when you can display it in an embellished stamped mat? Here, our sweet dog Daisy gets the setting she deserves.

Glass Plate Photo Frames

For an unusual way to display a photo, decoupage the back of a glass plate and include pretty scrapbook papers. Add a hanger to the back or set it on a miniature easel.

Storage Ideas

Sooner or later, every scrapbooker must confront one incontrovertible truth: You must either find an effective way to organize all those supplies or waste valuable time hunting down tools and materials. To create your custom storage solutions, start with a great functional product or re-purpose an item you already have, pull out your scrapbook supplies, and get to work.

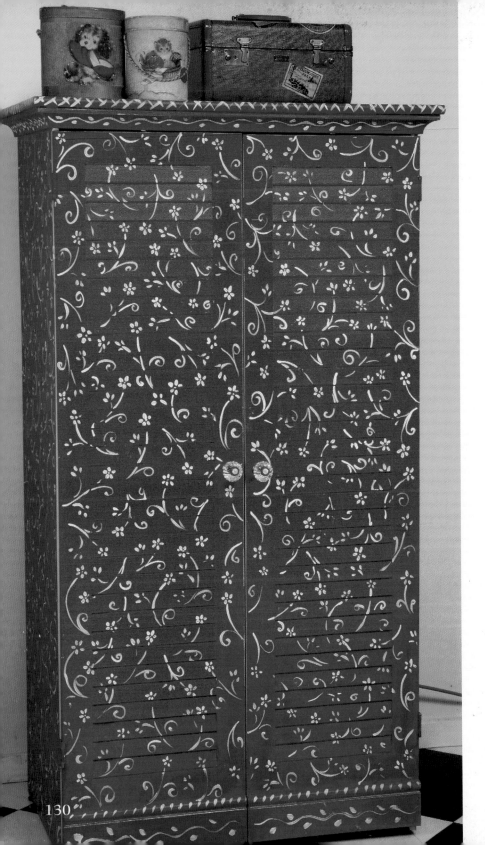

Scrapbooker's Armoire

I've always found that when my work space reflects the personality of my art, I'm more inspired. A store-bought cabinet with a foldaway table becomes my ideal craft center when covered with the sort of details I love. Mixing decorative objects in with functional features makes this a space I want to work in.

Easy Bulletin Board

Post inspirational images or a work-in-progress over your work space on a bulletin board that suits your decor. Made from foam-core board and fabric, this board is incredibly easy to build to whatever dimensions you need.

See project instructions on page 142.

Embellished Drawer System

Glue, tape, and small embellishments find a home in a melamine chest; but to me, the plain white surface was a bit too plain and a bit too white. Add a little bit of ribbon and few strips of paper and—ah, much better.

Ribbon Storage

Keep your ribbon like new in a jewelry case. The clear pockets on the case featured here lets you see at a glance what you have, and the hanger saves your valuable table space for projects.

Button Jar

Your project is almost done, and you just need one more bit of color, a spot of texture, a little something right *there*. In such moments, you can't go wrong when you reach for your trusty jar of buttons.

A Prettier Paper File

A melamine file box is a great place to store paper, inspiring magazines, and notes. I added paper polka dots, ribbons, paper flowers, and hand-drawn curlicues to make it clear that this one belongs to a scrapbooker.

Watchmaker's Cases

Small containers make small items easier
to find. If you're serious about your
embellishment collection, consider organizing
it in shallow aluminum containers with
clear lids like those used by watchmakers.

Flowerpot Storage

There's no need to buy fancy holders for scissors,
pencils, and other utensils when all you need is a
terra-cotta pot, some ribbon, a bit of paper, and
some cute embellishments.

Project Instructions and Materials

Party Time Present

Materials

- Two sheets of 12" x 12" scrapbook paper (Paper #1)
- Ruler
- Pencil
- Scissors
- Illustration board
- Spray adhesive
- Foam dots
- ½"-wide ribbon
- Double-sided tape
- One sheet of 12" x 12" scrapbook paper (Paper #2)
- Round paper tag
- "It's Party Time" sentiment
- Small hole punch
- 10" of string
- "Let's Celebrate" sentiment
- Linen Tape
- "Happy Birthday" sentiment

Directions

1. Make the present

Measure and cut an 8" x 8" square of Paper #1. Set aside scraps. Mount the square to the illustration board, using spray adhesive. Trim the illustration board to fit paper. Mount second sheet of Paper #1 to the back of the illustration board.

2. Make the lid

Cut a 1" x 8" strip of Paper #1 from the scraps of Step 1. Mount it to illustration board, using spray adhesive. Attach the strip to the top of the square, using foam dots. *Note: The top edge of the lid should be flush with the top edge of the square.*

3. Add ribbon

Measure and cut two equal lengths of ribbon for the corners of the present. Attach it to the square with double-sided tape. With additional ribbon, tie a bow. Set it aside.

4. Create the tag

Attach the "It's Party Time" sentiment to the round tag. Trim excess. Punch a small hole in the tag and tie to the bow with string. Attach the bow to the top of the present, using hot glue.

5. Attach the first sentiment

Center the "Let's Celebrate" sentiment ½" below the top of Paper #2. Glue in place.

6. Attach the present

Place the present face down with its top ½" below the "Let's Celebrate" sentiment. Tape the present to Paper #2 with a 7¾" strip of linen tape along the seam. Cover the tape with a strip of Paper #1, using spray adhesive.

7. Finish

Adhere your photo(s) and sentiments to Paper #2 (under the present) and, if you wish, to the back of the present itself.

Purse Album #1

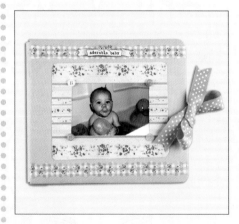

Materials

- 8½" x 9½" Pink album with brown edging
- One sheet of 12" x 12" scrapbook paper (Paper #1)
- Scissors
- Scallop scissors
- Decoapage medium

- A small craft brush for glue
- Plastic purse handle with flat ends
- Hot-glue gun with glue sticks
- One medium flower-shaped button
- One small round button
- Scrapbook paper (Paper #2)
- Flower punch
- Small rhinestones
- Woven "Smile" label
- Pom-pom trim
- Two 1¼"-wide clear self-adhesive page bubbles
- 6" of string
- Small hole punch

Directions

1. Make the purse

Place the album with its spine away from you. Create the purse flap by cutting a triangle from Paper #1. Scallop the bottom edge of the triangle. Adhere the flap to the top, using decoupage medium and a brush. Hot-glue the plastic purse handle behind the front cover. *Note: The Colorbök album style I used has a small pocket behind the front cover that makes this easy to do.*

2. Create the purse clasp

Hot-glue the flower button to the point of the purse flap. Hot-glue the round button to the center of the flower button.

3. Embellish the purse

Make paper flowers, using Paper #2 and the flower punch. Adhere them randomly across the purse, using decoupage medium and a brush. Hot-glue the

rhinestones to the center of each flower. Hot-glue the woven label to the front cover. Hot-glue the pom-pom trim to the bottom edge of the inside cover.

4. Finish

Cut and write the nametag on a disk of scrapbook paper, then place it between the self-adhesive page bubbles. Punch a small hole in the tag and attach it to the purse handle with string.

Cake Card

Materials
- Solid-colored cardstock
- Scissors
- Four small pieces of different scrapbook papers (Paper #1–Paper #4)
- Scallop scissors
- Scrapbook paper (Paper #5)
- Pinking shears
- Paper scraps (including a small piece of yellow paper)

- Craft glue stick
- Small beads, rhinestones, glitter, paper flowers, and bows
- Fine-tip paper craft glue
- Hot-glue gun and glue sticks

Directions

1. Create the card

Fold the cardstock and round the outer edges, using scissors. If using a ready-made envelope, test to see that the card will fit. *Note: The embellished card will fit more snugly.*

2. Prepare the cake layers

Cut one 1¼" x ¾" rectangle from Paper #1. Cut one 2" x ¾" rectangle from Paper #2. Cut one 2¼" x ¾" rectangle from Paper #3. Set them aside.

3. Prepare the cake plate

Cut Paper #4 into the following shapes: one thin rectangle (for the pedestal), one large hexagon (for the plate), and one small hexagon (for the base). Scallop the wide edges of the hexagons.

4. Prepare the frosting

Cut three strips of Paper #5 to the following dimensions: ³⁄₁₆" x 1½", ³⁄₁₆" x 2", and ³⁄₁₆" x 2¼". Cut the bottom edge of each strip, using pinking shears.

5. Prepare the candle

Cut a small, thin rectangle of any paper but Paper #5. Cut a tiny scrap of yellow paper for the flame.

6. Build the cake

Adhere the cake layers, cake plate, frosting strips, candle, and flame to the front of the card, using glue stick.

7. Embellish the cake

Attach tiny beads and glitter, using glue stick and/or fine-tip paper craft glue. Hot-glue larger embellishments such as bows.

Paper Purse Invitation

Materials

- Stiff scrap paper
- Pencil
- Ruler
- Scissors
- Envelopes
- Scrapbook paper (Paper #1)
- Illustration board
- Spray adhesive
- Scrapbook paper (Paper #2)
- Tape
- Pom-pom trim or ribbon
- Paper craft glue
- Large and small scallop scissors
- 1/8"-wide black or white trim
- Shoe cut from scrapbook paper
- Fine-tip glue
- Glitter

Directions

1. Make a pattern

Create a purse pattern for the basic card, using stiff scrap paper, pencil, and ruler. Make sure the purse will fit inside the envelopes you have chosen. *Note: Embellished paper will fit more snugly than plain paper.*

2. Prepare the card

Mount Paper #1 to the illustration board, using spray adhesive.

3. Trace the front of the purse

Place the purse pattern so that its wider end is against the edge of the mounted Paper #1. Trace.

4. Trace the back of the purse

Turn the purse pattern so that its narrow end is flush with the narrow end of the image you traced in Step 3. Trace. *Note: When you are finished with Step 3 and Step 4, you should have an hourglass-shaped outline.*

5. Cut the purse

Cut the bottom and outside edges of the purse shape, leaving the narrow ends connected. Fold the purse body so that it stands like a greeting card with the scrapbook paper facing out. Set it aside.

6. Cut the purse flap

Cut a triangle from Paper #2. Scallop two of its edges, using the small scallop scissors.

7. Attach the purse flap

Place the card front side up. Attach the top back side of the purse flap to the front of the card, using tape. *Note: The purse flap should hang free from the taped end.*

8. Make the handle

Cut 8" of pom-pom trim or ribbon. Glue or tape the ends under the purse flap. Secure the bottom point of the purse flap with a dot of glue.

9. Create a border

Cut a 3/4"-wide strip of Paper #2, using the large scallop scissors. Glue it to the bottom edge of the purse. Attach a trim that matches the handle along the border.

10. Finish

Glue a small pom-pom to the bottom point of the purse flap. Glue a cut-out shoe or boot embellishment in the center of the flap. Glue trim over the seams of the card. Trace free-form designs across the purse with fine-tip glue and sprinkle with glitter.

Love Bar Party Favors

Materials
- Six large chocolate bars
- Six sheets of coordinating scrapbook paper
- Scissors
- Sentiment tags
- Embellishments
- Ribbon
- Nontoxic glue

Directions

1. Prepare the wrappers
Remove the outer wrapping of each candy bar. Cut six new wrappers from different sheets of scrapbook paper, using an original wrapper as a template.

1. Attach the wrappers
Layer each new wrapper with strips of other papers and add ribbon, embellishments, and sentiment tags. Attach the wrappers to the chocolate bars, using nontoxic glue.

Elegant Glass Plates

Materials
- Two glass plates
- Wedding quote printed on vellum
- Bridal images
- Vines (fresh or paper)
- Flowers (fresh, pressed, and/or paper)

Directions

1. Decorate the bottom plate
Place the printed quote and bridal images on one plate. Scatter vines and flowers around the borders.

2. Finish
Set the second plate on top of the first. After the party, separate the plates and reuse the embellishments.

Sweety Cups

Materials
- Scrapbook papers (Paper #1 and Paper #2)
- Scissors
- Large scallop scissors
- 3¼"-tall solid-color paper cup
- Spray adhesive
- Large flower paper punch with thin petals
- Scrapbook paper (Paper #3 the same color as the cups)
- Paper craft glue
- Pom-poms
- Hot-glue gun and glue sticks

Directions

1. Prepare the bottom stripe
Cut a 2½"-wide strip of paper, using Paper #1 for half of the cups and Paper #2 for the remaining half. Scallop the top edge of each strip.

2. Attach the bottom stripe

Spray adhesive onto the back of the strip. *Note: Spray adhesive is toxic, so use it well away from the cups and be sure to apply it to the strips, not the cups themselves.* Apply one strip to each of the cups, leaving a ¼" overhang on the bottom. Cut darts into the overhang and fold the edges under evenly to create a smooth base.

3. Cut the flowers

Punch flowers for half your cups from Paper #1. Repeat, using Paper #2. Set these flowers aside in one group. Create a second group by punching flowers for all the cups from Paper #3.

4. Attach the flowers

Place one flower from the first group (made from Paper #1 or #2) on top of one flower from the second group (made from Paper #3) so that the petals alternate. Adhere together with paper craft glue. Hot-glue a pom-pom to the center of the. Hot-glue the finished flower to a cup. Repeat to embellish all the cups.

Recipe for Relaxation Envelope

Materials

- Two kinds of 12" x 12" scrapbook paper (Paper #1 and Paper #2)
- Scissors
- Ruler
- Pencil
- Scallop scissors
- Cardstock
- Clear-drying paper glue
- ⅜"-wide ribbon
- Glass cabochon
- Ink pen
- Large paper flower
- Hot-glue gun and glue sticks
- Double-sided tape

Directions

1. Begin the envelope

Cut Paper #1 into two 6" x 12" strips. Set one strip aside. Fold the other strip in half to form a square. Measure and cut Paper #2 into two ¾" x 12" strips.

Scallop the long sides of the Paper #2 strips. Fold the scalloped strips in half so they are 6" long.

2. Seal the envelope

Place the square so that the folded end is away from you. Seal the left-hand side of the square by gluing the right lower quarter of a scalloped strip along the border. Flip the square and glue the rest of the scalloped strip to seal one side of the envelope. Repeat for the remaining side. *Note: Glue the two scalloped borders close the sides of the envelope, leaving the top open.*

3. Embellish the envelope

Glue ribbon along the top border of the envelope. Write a word such as "Spa" on a scrap of Paper #2. Glue a cabochon over the word. Trim excess paper. Hot-glue the cabochon to the center of a large paper flower. Hot-glue the flower to the center of the envelope. Attach the envelope to a chair, using ribbon or double-sided tape.

4. Make the ribbon hanger

Cut two 2"-long strips from ribbon. Attach both end of one strip to the inside top edge of the envelope to form a loop. Repeat on the remaining side. Cut two strips from 10"-long ribbon. Tie one end of a longer ribbon to a loop. Repeat on the remaining side. Tie the loose ends of the longer ribbons together in a bow. Trim off the excess.

5. Create recipe cards

Fold, score, and tear 3" x 4" rectangles of cardstock. Write or attach copies of spa recipes on each card. Tuck the cards into the envelope.

Napkin Rings

Materials

- Scrapbook paper
- Illustration board
- Ruler
- Pencil
- Scissors
- Spray adhesive
- Clamp-style paper clip
- Retro-style labels with images of food
- Pinking Shears
- Nontoxic paper craft glue

Directions

1. Create the ring

Mount scrapbook paper to illustration board, using spray adhesive. Measure and cut the mounted paper into 1¼" x 6½"

strips. Close each strip to form a circle, design side out. Glue and hold closed with a paper clip until dry.

2. Embellish

Cut the edges of the retro-style labels, using pinking shears. Attach a label to the center of each ring, using nontoxic glue.

Dog Basket Centerpiece

Materials

- Flat-sided container (no wider than 8")
- Four sheets of 12" x 12" scrapbook paper (Paper #1)
- Illustration board
- Spray adhesive
- Pencil
- Scissors
- Four black pom-poms
- Hot-glue gun and glue sticks
- One sheet of 12" x 12" scrapbook paper (Paper #2)
- Four paper flowers
- 18" of ribbon

- Clear-drying paper glue
- Tape (optional)

Directions

1. Prepare Paper #1

Mount one sheet of Paper #1 to illustration board, using spray adhesive. Trim off excess illustration board. Mount a second sheet of Paper #1 to the back of the illustration board to create a sturdy, double-sided square. Repeat to create a second square.

2. Create silhouettes

Draw the profile of a dog on one square. *Note: Make sure the dog is as long as your flat-sided container is wide.* Cut it out. Trace the cut-out silhouette on the second square. Cut out the second silhouette.

3. Add the nose

Hot-glue one pom-pom on each side of the two silhouettes.

4. Make the collar

Cut four strips from Paper #2. Glue one strip on each side of the dog. Hot-glue the paper flowers.

5. Assemble the basket

Hot-glue one silhouette to a side of your container. Repeat.

6. Create the handle

Mount one sheet of Paper #2 to another, using spray adhesive. Cut two 1" x 12" strips from the double-sided

Paper #2. Glue one end of each strip to the inside rim of your container.

7. Finish

Glue or tape the loose ends of the strips to form a handle. Cover the seam at the top by tying your ribbon around the handle to form a bow.

Domed Photo Display

Materials

- Photo (slightly larger than the top of the bowl)
- Mat board
- Spray adhesive
- Small clear glass bowl
- Pencil
- Scissors
- Embellishments
- Photo-safe glue
- Hot-glue gun and glue sticks
- 1"-wide linen tape
- Round hanger
- Ribbon

Directions

1. Create the base

Mount the photo on the mat board, using spray adhesive. Place the bowl upside down on the mounted photo. Trace the circumference and cut out the circle. Glue embellishments to the photo, using photo-safe glue.

2. Attach the bowl to the base

Apply hot glue to the rim of the bowl. Press the embellished photo into place. Let the glue set. Cut a strip from linen tape long enough to circle the bowl. Cut darts into the tape. Apply the tape to the rim to cover the glue line.

3. Finish

Hot-glue the hanger to the back of the base. Secure the hanger with a small strip of linen tape. Thread ribbon through the hanger and tie in a knot or bow at the top.

Easy Bulletin Board

Materials

- ¼"-thick foam-core board
- Utility knife
- Ruler
- Pencil
- Sturdy fabric
- Scissors
- Spray adhesive
- Rickrack (enough for perimeter of board)
- Fabric adhesive
- Four upholstery tacks (4)
- Tack hammer

Directions

1. Prepare the board

Cut foam-core board slightly smaller than desired dimensions, using utility knife. Cut fabric so that it will cover the board with a 2" overhang on each side. *Note: If you cut the corners of the fabric, you will minimize bunching in Step 2.*

2. Apply the fabric to the board

Spray the fabric with adhesive. Spread it smoothly over the board. Fold the corners, sides, and edges toward the back of the board. Apply the rickrack border, using fabric adhesive.

3. Attach the board to the wall

Spray the back of the board; press it to the wall. Secure it with a tack in each corner.

 *Thank You*

It's a great time to be a designer. Crafters are interested in doing so many different types of projects in so many different styles that people like me get to work constantly on devising new concepts, products, and designs. It's invigorating, I love it, and I couldn't do it without you. Thank You.

Acknowledgments

Thank you to the following people for their help with this book:

To Blumenthal Lansing for my favorite buttons

To the people at Colorbök …
> Bill Taylor for believing in me and manufacturing this wonderful line of scrapbooking materials
> Colleen MacDonald for her design vision
> Aimee Walter for her seemingly endless and tireless graphic design expertise
> The Colorbök staff for helping with a few of the pages
> Colorbök for the albums, paper kits, sentiments, card kits, mini album kits and 3D embellishments

To Fiskars for the fantastic punches and decorative scissors

To Offray for great contemporary ribbons

To Plaid for the hip rubber stamps

To Prima for pretty paper flowers

To Sauder for the great craft armoire

To my friends and family who appear in the photos …
> The beautiful Parrague family for appearing in the mini album kits
> Taylor Vandevoir for her theatrical poses (she's the baby with rubber ducky in her mouth)
> Pam, Darla, Sharon, Heidi and Sara for being my Spa Party guests
> Danny, Buddy and Ruby for being my Dog Party guests All the members of my family who allowed me to use their photos

To the people at Chapelle …
> Jo, your enthusiasm and laugh are contagious—you are a joy!
> Ryne, you outdid yourself with these lovely photographs
> Jenn Gibbs, my favorite writer, you are a delight

To the people at Dena Designs …
> Heidi and Sara, I can't ever thank you enough—such talent!

To my sweet children for appearing again and again in this book, and for putting up with me and the huge messes I made creating these projects

To Dad for truly being the most wonderful father imaginable

To Mom—you're the babe and you continue to amaze me

To my husband Danny—the biggest hug and kiss for being everything to me

Metric Conversion Charts

inches to millimeters and centimeters							yards to meters										
inches	mm	cm	inches	cm	inches	cm	yards	meters	yards	meters	yards	meters	yards	meters	yards	meters
⅛	3	0.3	9	22.9	30	76.2	⅛	0.11	2⅛	1.94	4⅛	3.77	6⅛	5.60	8⅛	7.43
¼	6	0.6	10	25.4	31	78.7	⅛	0.11	2⅛	1.94	4⅛	3.77	6⅛	5.60	8⅛	7.43
½	13	1.3	12	30.5	33	83.8	¼	0.23	2¼	2.06	4¼	3.89	6¼	5.72	8¼	7.54
⅝	16	1.6	13	33.0	34	86.4	⅜	0.34	2⅜	2.17	4⅜	4.00	6⅜	5.83	8⅜	7.66
¾	19	1.9	14	35.6	35	88.9	⅝	0.46	2½	2.29	4½	4.11	6½	5.94	8½	7.77
⅞	22	2.2	15	38.1	36	91.4	⅝	0.57	2⅝	2.40	4⅝	4.23	6⅝	6.06	8⅝	7.89
1	25	2.5	16	40.6	37	94.0	¾	0.69	2¾	2.51	4¾	4.34	6¾	6.17	8¾	8.00
1¼	32	3.2	17	43.2	38	96.5	⅞	0.80	2⅞	2.63	4⅞	4.46	6⅞	6.29	8⅞	8.12
1½	38	3.8	18	45.7	39	99.1	1	0.91	3	2.74	5	4.57	7	6.40	9	8.23
1¾	44	4.4	19	48.3	40	101.6	1¼	1.03	3¼	2.86	5⅛	4.69	7¼	6.52	9⅛	8.34
2	51	5.1	20	50.8	41	104.1	1¼	1.14	3¼	2.97	5¼	4.80	7¼	6.63	9¼	8.46
2½	64	6.4	21	53.3	42	106.7	1⅜	1.26	3⅜	3.09	5⅜	4.91	7⅜	6.74	9⅜	8.57
3	76	7.6	22	55.9	43	109.2	1½	1.37	3½	3.20	5½	5.03	7½	6.86	9½	8.69
3½	89	8.9	23	58.4	44	111.8	1⅝	1.49	3⅝	3.31	5⅝	5.14	7⅝	6.97	9⅝	8.80
4	102	10.2	24	61.0	45	114.3	1¾	1.60	3¾	3.43	5¾	5.26	7¾	7.09	9¾	8.92
4½	114	11.4	25	63.5	46	116.8	1⅞	1.71	3⅞	3.54	5⅞	5.37	7⅞	7.20	9⅞	9.03
5	127	12.7	26	66.0	47	119.4	2	1.83	4	3.66	6	5.49	8	7.32	10	9.14
6	152	15.2	27	68.6	48	121.9										
7	178	17.8	28	71.1	49	124.5										
8	203	20.3	29	73.7	50	127.0										

Index

4/10   25   1/10
7/12   (27) 2/11
2/17 (35) 10/15